spot

AFRICAN ANIMALS

HIPPOS

by Mary Ellen Klukow

AMICUS | AMICUS INK

nostrils

teeth

Look for these
words and pictures
as you read.

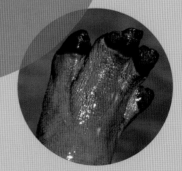

skin

foot

What's that in the water?
It's a hippo!

Hippos live in the river.
They live in a group
called a herd.

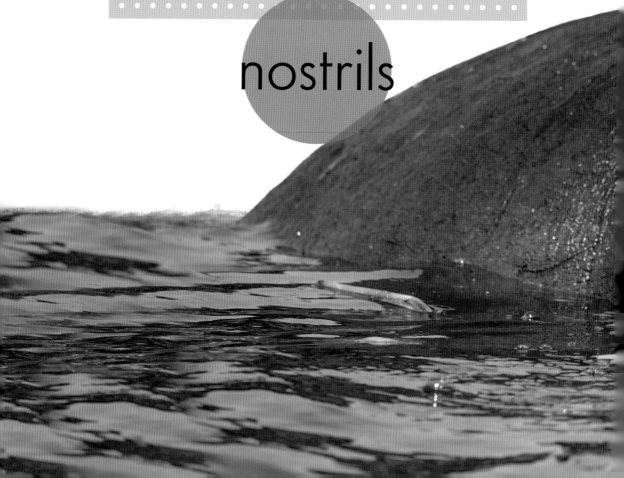

Look at the nostrils.
They can close.
Hippos can hold their
breath for five minutes!

nostrils

Look at the teeth.
They never stop growing.
Hippos have 36 teeth.

teeth

Look at the skin.
It can be 2 inches (5 cm) thick.

skin

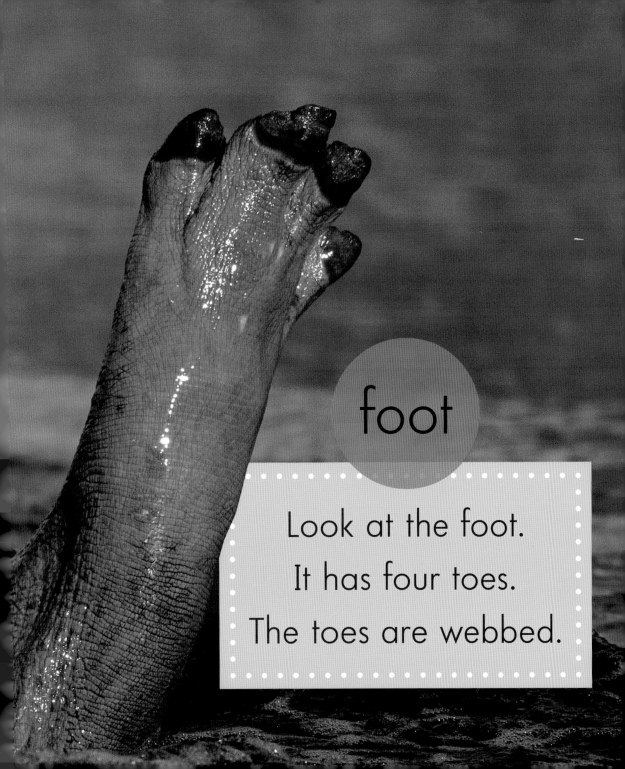

foot

Look at the foot.
It has four toes.
The toes are webbed.

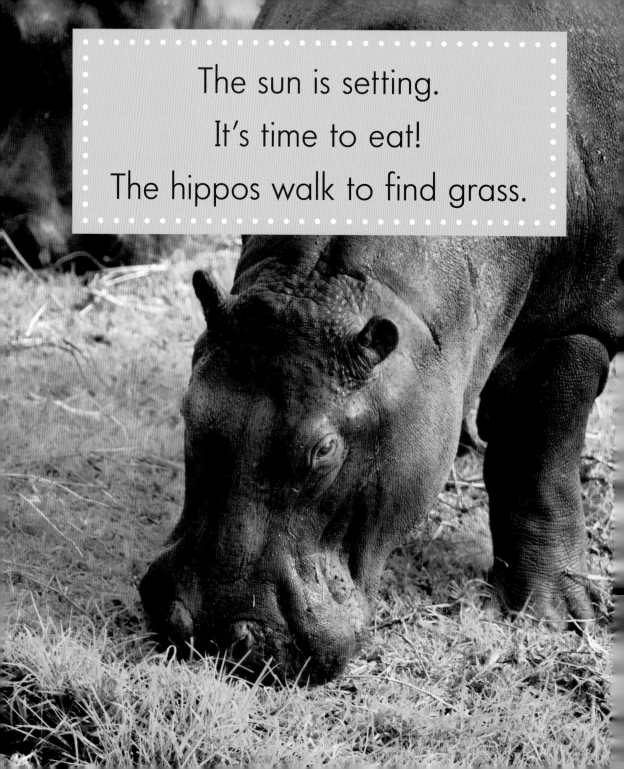

The sun is setting.
It's time to eat!
The hippos walk to find grass.

Look at the nostrils.
They can close.
Hippos can hold their
breath for five minutes!

nostrils

Look at the teeth.
They never stop growing.
Hippos have 36 teeth.

teeth

nostrils

teeth

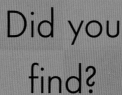

Did you
find?

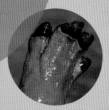

skin

foot

Look at the skin.
It can be 2 inches (5 cm) thick.

skin

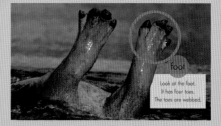

foot

Look at the foot.
It has four toes.
The toes are webbed.

Spot is published by Amicus and Amicus Ink
P.O. Box 1329, Mankato, MN 56002
www.amicuspublishing.us

Library of Congress Cataloging-in-Publication Data
Names: Klukow, Mary Ellen, author.
Title: Hippos / by Mary Ellen Klukow.
Description: Mankato, Minnesota : Amicus, [2020] | Series:
   Spot. African animals | Audience: K to Grade 3. |
Identifiers: LCCN 2018025826 (print) | LCCN 2018031223
   (ebook) | ISBN 9781681517230 (pdf) | ISBN
   9781681516417 (library binding) | ISBN 9781681524276
   (paperback) | ISBN 9781681517230 (ebook)
Subjects: LCSH: Hippopotamidae--Africa--Juvenile literature.
Classification: LCC QL737.U57 (ebook) | LCC QL737.U57
   K58 2020 (print) | DDC 599.63/5--dc23
LC record available at https://lccn.loc.gov/2018025826

Printed in China

HC   10 9 8 7 6 5 4 3 2 1
PB   10 9 8 7 6 5 4 3 2 1

Wendy Dieker, editor
Deb Miner, series designer
Ciara Beitlich, book designer
Holly Young, photo researcher

Photos by iStock/pjmalsbury cover;
Shutterstock/Eric Isselee 1; iStock/
brytta 3; iStock/narvikk 4–5; iStock/
USO 6–7; Getty/Mint Images/Art
Wolfe 8–9; Getty/Manoj Shah 10–11;
Minden/Richard Du Toit 12–13; iStock/
nicolamargaret 14

HIPPOS